The **PIOOYA** Principles

The 21ˢᵗ Century's Ultimate

Anti-Self-Help Book

D1190374

By Nehrwr Abdul-Wahid and Bill Mease

ISBN 978-0-557-98074-1

Introduction

The Legend

In a narrow valley shielded by a maze of ice fields and volcanic peaks lies the simple hamlet of Boopas, Iceland. As a few dedicated sojourners descend into the hamlet they are immersed in an odd, but pleasant sensation. Each breath senses an energized calmness. In the field below, surrounded by an intensely focused group of visitors, stands a slightly built 97-year old farmer, Oyu Piooya (pronounced, "pie-ooh-yah"). Piooya, *the hamlet's healer and spiritual guide is the magnet that draws travelers across the inhospitable terrain to the gentle fields of the valley.*

In the spring of 2008 the authors, along with 4 other colleagues, had the opportunity to visit and learn from this unimposing, yet powerful farmer what was described to us as the **Piooya Principles.** *We had heard about these principles through a well-respected teacher and mentor, Dr. Ero Cruttures, before her untimely passing just weeks before our trip. Fortunately, she provided us with detailed information on how to* *locate Oyu. In honor of our mentor Dr. Cruttures, we had decided to make the trip.*

Our experience with Oyu Piooya was profoundly liberating. Suffice it to say that being in the presence of a spirit so free, yet so connected to the earth, left each of us with greater possibilities for a life well lived.

Oyu shared with us that, in accordance with tradition, he had divulged only what we could absorb. "A life of excess is a life of waste", was oft repeated to his impatient American guests. Receiving subsequent lessons depended wholly on our ability to transform these initial lessons into actions that would bear fruit for the benefit others.

Oyu gave us his blessing to share these principles with anyone who wanted them. In his final words, he prepared us for the reality of our return, "many will listen, few will hear, take heart in that this must be so."

We are hopeful, yet have no idea who will listen and who will hear.

Our mission is simply to forward the message of the PIOOYA Principles.

<u>Note to reader</u>:

If you believe that what you just read is true, the rest of this book is for you. What you just read is fiction. There is an Iceland, but there is no Boopas. There is no Oyu. There was no sojourn with colleagues. Why would we create the story?

Here's why.

People love to look for the answers to life's mysteries in exotic places. Or where it's easiest…like looking for their lost keys under the streetlight but on a road they've never been on. When you ask them why they're looking there, they answer, "because the light's better here!"

Aren't we all tired of the barrage of experts telling us that the key is out there, somewhere. As much as we would like to believe this, it simply is not true. Each of us, in his or her own way, has to go **inside,** <u>not</u> <u>outside</u> - to find our path.

The Real Story

There is no one. And that includes us, the authors of this piece and the experts we all paid last year to provide some insight and answers. No matter how strange the name, no matter how exotic the location, no matter what the degree or letters before and/or after the name, no matter how ancient the wisdom and no matter how well guarded the "secrets" – no one has the answers for the tough choices in your life or ours. In fact, we have something surprising in common, you don't have the answers for us, and we don't have the answers for you. What we do have to offer are principles, time and experience tested guideposts to help us navigate the extraordinary event called our life.

Our reasons for writing this little piece and the circumstances of its birth are much more modest. We were grinding through a curriculum design meeting for an upcoming retreat with some colleagues. We were at that point in the creative process where all seemed lost, nothing appeared to fit and everyone was close to folding their tents and heading home.

It was precisely at that point, someone asked, "well, what are we going to do if none of this works?" The silence was as thick as the Minnesota snow covering the ground. We looked at one another for an answer...**the** answer. We were in what we have decided to call 'the brief pause for the moment of crashing insight.' Finally, one of us spoke up, "you'll do what you always do...pull it out of your ass." Aha! The universe has heard our plea and delivered not the answer, but the cosmic question. How can we consciously repeat those wonderful experiences when surprised, baffled and frustrated by circumstance we muster our personal magic and meet the challenge with resounding success?

What if we could increase the moments in every day that we live with freedom, fearlessness and confidence. What if we could repeat the joy, magic and downright thrill of all of those times we've just pulled it out of our ass? We could approach each day, with all its uncertainty, immersed in an extraordinary spirit unspoiled by arrogance. If we walked through every situation in our lives knowing we could handle whatever is thrown at us, wouldn't that be the ultimate source of freedom?

Yet – isn't that *exactly* what we do? Not every moment, not frequently enough – but indeed we do. We do it when we've spent the last week preparing a presentation for the boss and the night before our computer crashes. The faint-hearted call in sick. The *PIOOYA Masters* walk in and make do!

We do it when we can't find the correct size c-clamp to use on that water pump and we have to be at work in 30 minutes. Some of us find some duct tape, maybe even that necktie you bought your husband for his birthday (he never liked it anyway) – and somehow, we make it work.

Adopting these principles is about reconnecting with our human history. If our ancestors weren't **PIOOYA Masters**, then there is no such thing! They made wheels out of boulders, fire out of clicking a couple stones, tools out of branches and rocks, homes out of a vision, and whole cities out of rubble!

In our design meeting we had walked smack into the timeless mother of invention…obstacle blocking destination. When push came to shove we would make "it" work, whatever "it" was! The search for the **PIOOYA Principles** began that day.

This was not the birth of a babe on its way to Harvard…**PIOOYA Principles** are grounded in the reality of our every day lives. Modest beginnings belie the power of simplicity. If you read and practice these principles we're willing to make some extraordinary guarantees.

Our Guarantees

We guarantee that the **PIOOYA Principles** will not help you live your dreams. Dreams realized are no longer dreams - they're your life! This is why we vastly overrate the happiness so many "things" or achievements will bring us. That new car or perfect relationship soon become "the car" and "a-work-in-progress." Living the dream happens only with the aid of some serious chemical use.

We guarantee that the **PIOOYA Principles** will not suddenly unleash all of your incredible potential. (We don't know you, maybe you're already close enough for comfort). But remember, each mountain-top provides a more expansive view. Possibilities for our lives aren't dropped on our doorstep in a single UPS delivery. They arrive as past experiences position us to see them.

We guarantee that the **PIOOYA Principles** will not eliminate pain and suffering from your life. There's nothing more worrisome, and perhaps dangerous, than a perpetually grinning recent convert to anything. The pain of living this life may come in sharp surges or dull throbs, but it will come. There is no preemptive move. Constant trips to the mall, the bar, and video games are only temporary distractions.

Let's take it one step further. And please notice how you react to the following statement:

We guarantee that you have already thought of pretty much everything we are going to say. That's the beauty of it! We're already on the same page. Seeing what we've all seen, but with new eyes...the core of innovation.

The beauty of the **PIOOYA Principles** is that they don't promise more than they can deliver. What they can deliver are more *moments* of deep gratitude, full laughter, profound peace, energized passion and expansive love.

A Decency Disclaimer

If you haven't made the connection between "pull it out of your ass" and the PIOOYA Principles...you should probably turn the TV off while you're reading. Just a thought.

We use PIOOYA as short-hand. In the end (pun intended) what we're talking about is using what we already have with what we already know (and don't know) to get us where we want to go.

From time to time we may be distracted by random shiny objects, slip into metaphors, stories or general weirdness. This simply mimics life for all of us. Through all of the distractions and detours we're hoping to join you in the search for a path that leaves as little potential behind as possible.

PIOOOYA PRINCIPLES: SUMMARY

We've never understood why as readers we have to work our way through an entire written piece to figure out how it all fits together. We present the summary below so that you can see the map, relax and spend the rest of the time applying and adding your own pieces to the puzzle.

PIOOYA Principles free up energy by lifting the heavy veil of some seriously hyped myths. And what is a Myth? It's a false idea or belief shared by the masses.

Why would the masses believe something that's false?

Because societies need a narrative to hold together, a story that outlines good and bad behavior and the consequences for both. Truth is less important than function here, although if questioned, most would declare that the myth was the truth. To work outside of this myth is to be outside the society itself. (And nobody likes being the outsider…except the group of outsiders that create a new group where they're the insiders!)

Myths create a mindset. In America there was a time when those whose skin color was black were property, not human beings. All myths dictate what is and is not possible. The myth above created a sense of superiority and privilege on the part of slave owners and inferiority on the part of slaves. Myths provide the rationale for what's right, what's wrong and more importantly, who's right and who's wrong.

Myths guide behavior. In many cases they justify outrageous behavior as in the myth above, but they also provide rationales for acceptable behavior throughout society. They do so by providing meaning to events. A television preacher decided that the earthquakes that decimated Haiti were God's punishment for worshipping the devil.

Ultimately, myths provide a structure for society to function. Some argue that myths only harm a society. Others say that they serve a lot of good in determining acceptable and unacceptable behavior. They most likely do both depending upon one's perspective. The only time we want to debunk a myth is when it gets in the way of individual possibility.

PIOOYA Mastery is nothing more than our ancestral language of freedom.

When you follow **PIOOYA Principle 1**, Problem, Not Catastrophe, you enjoy the freedom of *no longer living under the myth of "immanent catastrophes"*. This frees up all the energy sucked up by being constantly on red alert. That energy can now focus on a path forward.

As you adopted **PIOOYA Principle 2**, It's Up to You, you freed yourself from the *myth that you can control your destiny* and focused on what you can control, your decisions and commitment to them. Getting in sync with what's truly up to you and what isn't plants your feet firmly in the soil of reality.

PIOOYA Principle 3, Own Your Limitations, frees us from the myth that both having and acknowledging limitations is a weakness in itself. Instead, by *acknowledging our limitations* we strengthen the options we have for making great decisions and wise commitments.

In **PIOOYA Principle 4**, Only Moments Count, we make an extraordinary change. We switch the basic unit of perception in our lives. Instead of looking at days, weeks or years we focus on moments. Why? Because days, weeks and years are nothing more than long strings of moments. Improve the quality of moments and you've improved a lifetime. By avoiding the *myth that multi-tasking works* we can focus on creating moments that matter, for ourselves, the community and world we live in.

PIOOYA Principle 5, "You are ordinary and that is extraordinary" takes the pressure off. We're all electro-chemical, self-observing, future seeking, miracles…that's our starting line. Eliminating the myth that the action is somewhere else frees us up to experience gratitude for the extraordinary life we're living and possibilities of our life yet unlived.

The final principle between you and **PIOOYA Mastery** is Principle 6, that "authenticity *is* the action" which frees you from trying to prove to people that you are not what you did in that moment. You are! By accepting this truth, you are acknowledging the fullness of who you are with all of its contradictions.

PIOOYA Principle #1

"Problem, NOT catastrophe"

Myth: Catastrophe is just around the corner

Digging Deeper

<u>In the Beginning</u>

Ever since we popped our frightened heads outside the cave we've been wired to sense and assume catastrophe. Our ears tune out familiar sounds, but pick up unfamiliar noises in an instant. Our eyes automatically lock in on unanticipated movement. We can distinguish between friend or foe by smell alone. We have one goal...avoid being dinner. If that's a wooly mammoth crashing through the bushes after us, or a disgruntled uncle Ort heaving a boulder at us, it automatically garners our full attention.

Being pretty much the smallest, weakest kid on the prehistoric block we were on perpetual red alert. Unless you were in our immediate family you couldn't be trusted and even if you were - your ineptness could get us all killed. There simply was no guaranteed safe haven.

To avoid being lunch for Tyrannosaurus Rex, we needed to be superb threat detectors...and we were. So much so that it's embedded in the limbic system of our brain. Basically, we are wired to avoid being eaten by monsters and the wiring hasn't changed that much over time. In fact, we've simply developed another layer on top of the old cave man brain. Despite upgrading from the caves to our condos and big houses in the suburbs, what has happened to that immanent catastrophe warning system (ICWS)? Not much. It's still working twenty four seven. The big difference now is that most of the catastrophes are as imagined as the monsters we created as children (with the sole purpose to weasel into our parents beds). You remember those monsters under the bed or in the closet that gave you nightmares as a kid? As adults we've morphed those monsters into "catastrophes" lurking just around the corner. We may have difficulty describing them, but generally, it's that sense that danger is immanent. As if our built-in Immanent Catastrophe Warning System isn't enough we have the ongoing onslaught of the external version....24-hour worldwide news coverage.

The Immanent Catastrophe Feeder System

Entire industries depend on convincing us that a catastrophe is lurking just around the corner. Politicians promise to save us from the terror they spend so much time instilling. The military, whose funding depends upon the "constant threat" scenario, reminds us (in this case it's no myth) that there are people trying to kill us. Some of us still recall the elementary school drill of putting our hands behind our neck and getting under our desks to avoid being killed by the bomb the Russians were soon going to hurl at us. Even then it occurred to some that these must be the strongest little writing desks in the world if we're counting on them to stop the bomb from killing us.

As memorable as those times were, they are nothing compared with the most pervasive and aggressive of all, the *news terrorists*. Fear is right up there with sex on the "what sells" chart...a fact well noted by our major news organizations. There's good chance this next generation of kids will imagine Wolf Blitzer under their beds as opposed to the large green monsters of Yore. From CNN to FOX News, ratings depend on whether we're frightened enough to tune in ad infinitum. If you have a "Situation Room" there must be a "situation", right? But they're not alone, corporations scare us too. How many warrantees have we actually made full use of? And when something does actually go wrong with that big screen t.v., oh well, the warranty has either expired or doesn't cover what we need it to.

Wired for catastrophe on the inside and bombarded with apocalyptic messages from the outside—it's no wonder we're catastrophe junkies.

Catastrophe Revisited

The word "catastrophe" comes from the Greek word 'katastrophe', "kata" meaning down and "strophe" meaning turning. So what we fear is a sudden down turning. We fear it in a million forms. Instead of being eaten by a monster, which we would have to agree is a serious down turning - today it's a down-turning in our financial situation, health, social status, divorce, weight gain, cancer, hair loss, child unhappiness, bad prom date, TV not working….the list is endless. The first step in becoming a PIOOYA master is to accept that the power of catastrophe is in its imagined immanence. Let us repeat that. The challenge is to accept that the catastrophe just around the corner is in fact *a myth!* The power of catastrophe is in its imagined immanence, not in its occurrence. How could this be?

It's a matter of power. Powerlessness breeds anxiety. Anxiety shows up as everything from worry to panic attacks. We are absolutely powerless to do anything about an event that we are imagining as immanent. It's like battling a ghost…there is nothing to get your arms around. Doing something to impact a situation provides a sense of control. That is simply not an option when that something is an imagined event…an event that does not exist. This is why the real power of catastrophe is in its imagined immanence.

About 99.9% of feared catastrophes simply don't occur. But, don't get us wrong here. There are what we can call "catastrophic events." Real catastrophes like a life threatening illness, loss of a loved one, victimization by rape or incest – these all happen daily in thousands of lives. These lives will not be the same after the catastrophe. There is suffering. We have an entire belief system, Buddhism, based on this reality. But when in it (suffering), we address it. When catastrophe becomes reality, when it stops being an imagined immanent event, we tap our deepest resources and do what we always do, live our lives as well as we can. We actually exert some control over the situation, no matter how limited, which gives us a sense of some power and control.

Here is the core of the **First PIOOYA Principle**. When we shed our ancient reaction to "imagined immanent catastrophe" we free ourselves of endless hours of cowering in front of a paper tiger. That paper tiger may take the form of worry, anxiety, depression, even anger. All of these symptoms strip the freedom and quality from our lives.

Problem - NOT Catastrophe

Why is there no catastrophe? Because the challenge is here… it's happening *now*. It is neither imagined nor immanent, it's right in our face. The terrifying imagined immanence that left us powerless has been replaced with a challenging reality that we can in large or small measure have an impact on. Our power is back. A sense of some control, be it attitude or action, returns. Why? Because we *solve* problems, we get therapy for catastrophes!

And who do you need to say "problem, NOT catastrophe" to the most? Yup, you guessed it - yourself. Every time the worry or anxiety of imagined immanent catastrophe rears its primitive little head say the words with firm conviction, "It's just another problem, NOT a catastrophe – and I SOLVE PROBLEMS". Is this a path to massive delusion? Possibly. (See legal disclaimer regarding psychotic episodes caused by reading this material. In short, your problem, not ours.) However, it also may be a giant step into both reality and possibility.

There is no magic pill! There is no special sauce! There aren't 7,12, or 100 steps. There is ONE starting point– to accept your reality, stripped of false warnings, for all it is, the good, the bad and the in-between. Can we do it with confidence? Well, that's where the other five **PIOOYA Principles** come in. However, there is no moving forward to any of the other principles until one has fully mastered this most important step. So the question, before moving on, is… Is there a catastrophe waiting for you around the corner?

Well done! No catastrophe at all. Just a life event (another problem) we need to address. When we stop being surprised that the universe once again has failed to order itself in service to our perpetual glee we're on our way to PIOOYA mastery. We simply need to recognize that our *imagined* immanent catastrophes feed a powerlessness we need not participate in. When we are able to say "problem, NOT catastrophe – and I solve problems" our power is back! We are ready to travel the PIOOYA path.

Repeat after us: problem not catastrophe, problem not catastrophe; problem, not catastrophe; problem, not catastrophe… and I solve problems. Do you feel a little lighter? That's the freedom of PIOOYA seeping in. (Okay, if you didn't feel any lighter stand on your head for about 5 minutes. That should do it.)

So given that...who's gonna take care of the challenge?

You, that's who!

Imagined immanent catastrophe is no catastrophe at all.

PIOOYA PRINCIPLE 2

"IT'S UP TO YOU!"

The Myth

You are in control of your own destiny

Destiny: the events that **will** necessarily happen to a particular person or thing in the future.

Digging Deeper

What Exactly is "Up to You"

We are both terrified and astounded by the randomness of events.

Mother, father and three month old are in a tent in a campground. Elderly woman accidentally throws her car into reverse and panicked, freezes on the accelerator, backs over the tent, kills the three month old and cripples the mother.

A group of day laborers go in together on a lottery ticket. The ticket turns into a 50 million dollar bonanza.

In a quiet little Wyoming town a seventy nine year old celebrates the day with his wife. He had just gotten the news that he was finally cancer free. Hears a noise in the middle of the night. Bolts up in bed. Wife screams. Fifteen year-old burglar shoots him to death.

Driver falls asleep at the wheel and drifts across the rural highway. No one was coming the other way. He awakens suddenly and gets back on the right side.

Go figure. This is an average day on the planet! Throw in the randomness of life-ending disease, completely healthy new-borns, a Katrina or two, an oil spill, being accepted at a school one might have thought impossible and the myth just blows up on its own. Or does it?

With all this randomness, good and bad, how does the myth of being in charge of one's own destiny survive?

Why is this Myth So Tough to Crack?

Did you find yourself saying, "well, I don't camp, or fall asleep at the wheel and I do lock my doors and windows, so I'm good." If so, don't feel bad. We scurry around with lightening speed to differentiate ourselves from those who are the random targets of ill fortune. We simply cannot handle the anxiety caused by the randomness of events. Freddy have lung cancer? Please, please let him still be a smoker, because I quit long ago.

This myth is Teflon. It seems to endure against all odds (and data). In America, you can't get away from the myth that says you can be anything you want to be and achieve whatever you really decide you want to achieve, and oh, by the way, if you don't, well then that's *your* fault. It certainly serves a need for social control (stops the hordes of poor and middle class from grabbing their pitchforks and torches and heading for the nearest gated community). What it doesn't serve is reality. This myth is like America's junk food obsession. Who cares if it's clogging our arteries…it tastes soooo good!

Given your mastery of **PIOOYA Principle One** (yes, huge assumption, but hang with us for a sec), you are much better equipped to deal with reality, so let's do just that for a moment. For every cancer survivor who is a "fighter" there are many more who did not survive who were also "fighters". For every entrepreneur highlighted in the local paper there are many who labored for years and were unable to make it go. For every ten thousand aspiring actors or actresses who gave their heart and soul to be a star there are nine thousand nine hundred and ninety nine folks counting tips at the end of the night. And, how about your good fortune in staying healthy, having a job you like, and kids who are not serial killers?

There simply is no greater arrogance than taking credit for the results of random events.

Can we influence events in our lives? Yes. Can we plan wisely? Yes. Can we take care of ourselves physically and spiritually? Yes. Can we give our kids high expectations, love and helpful limits? Yes. Does all that make a difference? Yes. Can we stack the odds in our favor? Yes. Can we control our destiny? No!

So If We Don't Control Our Destiny, What Do We Control?

You can't apply the first PIOOYA Principle, Problem not catastrophe, without an understanding of the second, It's Up to You. If you say "Problem, not catastrophe" and believe you can control this little mini-destiny you're in for a remedial course in the dangers of delusion. (Remember, we're not liable for that.) So, what can we control? Our decisions and commitment to them.

Ghandi, who always strikes us as someone who might not have been a whole lot of fun to hang around with, maintained an absolute commitment to his decisions, no matter what the hardship. He won some. He lost some. He made a difference.

This myth of control of one's own destiny is destructive. Why? Because it narrows our vision. It represents a tunnel vision that simply cannot see the larger forces at work. It makes gratitude, humility and true connection almost impossible. If you believe your good fortune is due only to your work ethic you will certainly take an unfavorable view of those who have less good fortune. It simply makes you the implied center of the universe, larger than the forces of global, local or personal circumstance. The arrogance of it is not attractive, but, then again, beauty is in the eye of the beholder. The unrealistic nature of this view results only in an unsustainable grandiosity.

So, the big question is, "What exactly is up to me?" If you answered "destiny" fold the book up and take it back for a refund. (Which we've already covered will not be available.) What's up to you are *your decisions and commitment to them*. Want to add moments of joy and peace to your life? Make the shift from holding yourself accountable for destiny to holding yourself accountable for your decisions and the level of commitment to them. The difference is, the latter is consistent with what you can control and the other is a greasy slide into arrogance and delusion.

For example, you control whether you go to your son's football game or that business meeting. Of course, that assumes you didn't die in a car crash yesterday. Let's look at two options. Option A, you go to the business meeting and your son grows to appreciate how much time and energy you put into your job so that he can have some good shoulder pads and transportation to the game. Or, he hates you. Option B, you go to the game. Your son looks up in the stands and is gratified to see you there to watch him sit on the bench. Or, he hates you watching him fail. These are just four possibilities that come out of two options. Every day life presents thousands upon thousands of these possibilities. What did you control? Your decisions and commitment to them. What didn't you control, the outcome with your boss or your son.

Can you feel that? That's the weight of the world slowly being lifted off your shoulders. That's the feeling of PIOOYA in action.

These first two principles are nothing but good news. When you react to that sense of *imagined* immanent catastrophe for what it is, ancient wiring in need of a reality check, and respond with "Problem, no problem" you've set the foundation for change. When you re-align "It's up to you" in terms of decisions and commitment as opposed to destiny, you're ready to walk, feet firmly planted in reality, into any situation with the power of PIOOYA.

...Don't take credit or blame for lightning!

But don't go walking around with an iron rod in the middle of a thunderstorm either!

PIOOYA Principle #3

"Own Your Limitations"

Myth: Acknowledging limitations is a sign of weakness

Digging Deeper

<u>The Forces Against Owning Limitations</u>

We generally know how talented we are. Leave the fake humility at the cash register. We are well aware of how gifted we are. We also need to recognize and accept how talented *WE'RE NOT!*

Early on we had the ability to see our limitations and appeal to other sources, but somehow we lost it. Just spend a little time with any infant and it becomes dramatically clear. If the little fella wants food or a fresh diaper he has no qualms about sounding the siren that he needs a little help.

A few years later, the little tike would point up to the cupboard where the snacks were – letting you know in no uncertain terms what they wanted and who was responsible for getting it to them. Further down the path to independence they would quite readily ask for help with homework, or lunch, or dinner…and then all of the sudden…we're living with another adult (in the body of a 13-year old no less!)

There is a reality behind our refusal to own our limitations. We live in a culture that labels you "dinner" the moment you indicate there is something you are unable to do. It is seen as a weakness and weakness is something to be feasted on. As a result, some bad things happen. When traditional commercial banks started acting like hedge funds – the United State's financial health went in the tank. "Oops, forgot, we have no idea what we're doing but my check keeps getting bigger and bigger, whoopee."

Sometimes the force against owning your limitations is simply money. Make believe you can do it and someone will write you a check. While standing in a pool of water in our basement we realize we need help so we call the plumber. The *real* trouble begins when that plumber says "no problem" but has no idea why there's a pool of water in your basement! So rather than having the problem resolved, he's under your sink for 8 hours, charging you \$75/hr, because he's intent on tapping into his superior strengths at unclogging drains – as opposed to calling someone who knows how to solder a pipe!

The general perception is that owning up to limitations doesn't hold any rewards for most of us in our daily lives. It's almost un-American. Thousands and thousands of self help, motivational, how-to-be-a-better whatever books are out here on the shelves. (Which we now know simply don't work, with the exception of one of course - *the one you're reading*.) Driven, in part, by this insatiable thirst of Americans to know no limits. We can do *anything* we want to. Put our minds to it – put some elbow grease into it, roll up those sleeves – and we'll make it happen. In a room filled with voices screaming, "I can…pick me…I'm the one!" – to even *think* about anything less is considered career suicide.

How Does that Work, Turning Limitations into Strengths?

We've been running away from our limitations like a cancer rather than making full use of the antibodies inherent in them. They are great at repelling a big ego – which always spells disaster. Your ego said you could open up your laptop and replace the hard-drive yourself – and now your $1,500 replacement is a constant reminder to next time, tell your ego to shut the hell up why you go and get some help!

The ultimate freedom is the ability to see our limitations and their implications. The moment you acknowledge limitations they lose all of their power. It's amazing. That startling awareness that actually we aren't the only person on earth to be without limitations. And Limitations are a sign of our humanity rather than a weakness. You instantaneously have created a strength. In other words, something that you can now use to your benefit in becoming the person you want to be.

Don't go swimming in the ocean of your strengths without grabbing the lifejacket of your limitations. The sharks are circling.

It's one thing to acknowledge your limitations. It's another thing to use them as strengths.

Most of us in the solitude of our mental kingdoms suspect we have some limitations. It's the PIOOYA master who intentionally transforms these limitations into strengths. When we see a limitation we simply ask why it is so. Is it simply a technical limitation, something we don't know how to do? In that case we either connect with someone with different resources and get back to "problem, no problem" or, if time allows, we learn the new skill ourselves. Is it a limitation that comes in the form of a blind spot? If that's the case we will have to count on our most trusted friends and associates to help us see anew. Is it a limitation of attitude? If so, through self-reflection and loving relationships (and maybe some serious help) extricate or compensate our way out of a place we really don't want to be.

Can you see the theme? Our limitations, once acknowledged, drive us toward our humanity and a connectedness with others. It's dreadfully lonely out there for the Super-men and Wonder-women. They're simply inaccessible. Think of a time in your life when you felt you could finally do something for your parents that made a difference. You crossed the line of inaccessibility that often characterizes parent and child relationships and it felt wonderful. Increasing our accessibility and connectedness means we've transformed the cage into a platform for soaring.

...Remember, it's the space between the logs that fuels the fire

PIOOYA Principle #4

"Only moments count"

Myth: Multitasking Works

Digging Deeper

<u>Why don't we savor those moments?</u>

How many moments from yesterday do you remember? (If you're over sixty, try how many moments from today.) How about last week? If the pickings are slim you're not alone. We tend to have a "things will be better when…" mentality that takes us far away from approaching our lives through moments. Things will be better when…I find the right mate. Things will be better when…the kids are potty trained. Things will be better when…this diarrhea goes away.

There's nothing intrinsically wrong with looking forward to events, it's half the fun. The build up to the vacation trip, holiday, birthday or wedding is great. It does, however, carry two liabilities. First, except for the big anticipated event, we miss the 99.9% of our lives that lead up to it. Bad idea. Second, we lose track that what we do and how we choose to do it is a moment-by-moment choice we control. Moments are all we have…all we will ever have. And yet, we take no more notice of them than we do of the thousands of breaths that we take in an average day.

Let's take a mundane situation. You're on the phone with a credit card company trying to get them to eliminate the $5 penalty you feel was unfairly applied. Normally, you're annoyed at this waste of time and energy. Your annoyance turns into rudeness and ultimately anger, pretty much ruining your mood and the chance the ridiculous $5 fee will be removed from your bill.

When you adopt the principle that only moments count, you approach this as your choice. This isn't an interruption in what you want to do. This is what you've chosen to do, right here, right now – with this moment. You have to own and accept that as your choice! Having chosen this moment - you get to decide how you're going to be, and what you're going to do in it. You don't get to decide what will happen as a result of those choices! (remember **Piooya Principle #2)**

Life changes when you measure it in moments.

Generally, we are moment-less because we're operating in an unconscious fog of habit to either avoid the immanent catastrophe or rush hopefully toward our "happy place" we've built in the distant future. Neither one works for Piooya mastery. Piooya mastery demands a focus on right here and right now. If we are able to say, Problem, Not catastrophe, we had better be free enough to acknowledge our choices and tap our intuition. We feed that intuition by an all points radar scan for elements in the immediate moment that can be used to move us forward. This isn't as far- fetched as it may seem. Attending to emerging possibilities is in complete accordance with the relatively new science of self organizing systems and what is popularly known as chaos theory. (We threw this in for those wondering if we have ever read any related material or supporting research. We have not. We found this after a Google search on "stuff that sounds cool when trying to sound smart").

Look around at the pictures in your bedroom or office. Pictures are the wardens of moments. Seldom do we keep pictures of times and people we don't want to remember. Pictures literally capture a moment in time. That's why we keep them.

Look again at those pictures. Bet no one is multi-tasking.

What do we mean by multi-tasking doesn't work?
No one has ever made a memory worth keeping while they were multi-tasking...unless of course it was a car crash. No one, while multi-tasking, is aware of the moment and choices they are making. Couple this with some bad news from brain research...we actually can't multi-task. Research has determined that talking

on a cell phone is roughly the equivalent of driving while drunk in terms of accident probability. Apparently we're designed to only attend to one thing at a time. It turns out multi tasking is just a quick flickering of attention from one spot to another. So, every time you multi-task just chalk it up to moments in your life you didn't attend.

The important memorable times in our lives simply come when we are actually present, attending to one thing. To keep it simple we'll call it "Singling". (We're hoping to start a mass movement toward singling…our contribution to the twitter generation.) Can't you just see it now, you go to the cubicle of your co-worker for some help, because you were practicing Piooya Principle #3, and she says, "not now, I'm singling!" Obviously she's one chapter ahead.

It's amazing what happens to your life when you're "singling". Startle your spouse by giving him or her your complete, undiluted attention. Only drive when you're driving. Listen to music…that's all, just listen. Sit and read without the radio, TV or other background noise. Take turns sitting down with each of the kids. The opportunities for Singling are endless. You simply can't be a **Piooya Master** without being a Singler…and you don't need three years of meditation to do it.

Are we talking about Singling 24 hours a day? Ten? Five? Two? No, here's the good news, any moment you can spend Singling is a moment that provides a notch on your belt toward Piooya mastery. Moments of intimacy with a friend last forever, picture or no picture - they are moments in which we recognize we are in charge of how we're going to be and what we're going to do. They are moments of clarity, the fog of myth lifted.

While reading this chapter, were you Singling or multi-tasking?

We hope you made the moment count?

PIOOYA Principle #5

"You are ordinary...and THAT IS EXTRAORDINARY"

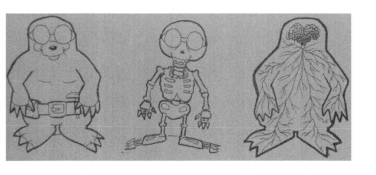

Myth: The action is somewhere else

Digging Deeper

<u>Your story *is* The Story</u>

Do you have any idea the amount of electrical energy produced by your mere lifting of that doughnut (that you know you shouldn't be eating!) Do you stop for a minute to reflect on the over 1 million receptors in each eye that translate reflective frequencies and make them into color pictures of the world around you or the words on this page? Yes – that boring world of yours sitting in the living room reading this book.

It may not feel that way, ***but the action is wherever you are***. The story your life is weaving continues every moment. But, we seldom notice. We need only visit the nearby grocery store to be reminded just how uninteresting our own lives are. Standing in the checkout line feeding our hunger to know who's marrying whom, who's leaving whom, and who else had a "prescription" drug problem (per their explanation for their troubled lives of fortunes lost).

Our obsession with the lives of others robs us of the recognition of the amazingness of our moments. Yes — those same moments you most recently reclaimed from the misguided notion that multi-tasking works. Now that you've recovered them, do you have any idea what you have?

We didn't. You probably don't either!

We've all been consumed with the five minutes of fame culture. Where actors have been replaced with regular Joe Schmoes and Suzy Q's on reality television and the criterion for writing a best seller these days has less to do with actual writing talent (thank God!) and more to do with how much abuse someone has suffered in their childhood. And recovering addicts can usually increase their book sales tenfold! (We might as well go public now that we both are addicted to pain killers and alcohol, have gambling problems and were severely emotionally traumatized that has left us scarred for life)

Cha-ching!

So why are we sitting at the table feasting on the smorgasbord of distraction? What do we see through the window of our neighbor that we don't have in our own home? (Okay, maybe it's a mid twenties hunk or starlet, but that's a different story.)

Chances are there is plenty of pain, suffering and disappointment in your lifetime (certain proof that you're not a sociopath and you are in fact conscious)– key ingredients to a great novel. Yet, there are also moments of triumph, love and real happiness.

You doubt?

Think back to the *moment* you learned to finally ride a bike. That moment! That sense of accomplishment and uncompromised victory.   Or how about that moment your mother surprised you with that birthday party when you thought everyone forgot. And when your lover (at *that* time) whispered in your ear that you were AMAZING! (okay, they were lying – but it sure felt good *in the moment!*) Those moments are all very significant.   Yet you insist on looking around…left and right…when you need look only in the mirror!

Do you know of a better story than someone who, when faced with a real catastrophe, channels their fear in such a way that they are able to tackle it head on and overcome whatever challenges present themselves? And while they confront whatever is in front of them, they are grounded in the reality of what they control, not destiny, but their decisions and commitment to them. They focus their energy toward whatever decision they make and follow through with it.   They embrace their limitations as strengths. So, rather than beating themselves up for being yet another imperfect human being, they embrace what they can't do and reach out for support. All the while, they make the most of each and every moment they have.

The fact that you often couldn't shake the sense that there's an imminent catastrophe waiting for you around the corner, yet, you still got up, everyday, and peeked around that corner, now THAT is extraordinary.

The fact that you know you could obey all the rules of the road, yet have no control over the other driver not paying attention who runs the red light and smashes into you. Yet, you still drive.

Doesn't that sound like a powerful biography of a modern-day hero?

That hero is you. This story is yours. You need only read it and continue to weave it.

Fascination with the cliff-notes of larger than life caricatures is like believing cartoon characters are real. Notice how the spotlight fades the more we learn about them.

Reality TV is a contradiction in terms. There is no reality on TV that holds a candle to yours. You are a chemical, electronic, atomic, soulful, feeling miracle! Piooya mastery holds that thought with humility, gratitude and a sense of responsibility.

…You are the book you have to read!

PIOOYA Principle #6

"Authenticity *is* the action!"

Myth: You *can* act outside your values

Digging Deeper

By the time you read this sentence, your body has gone through an infinite number of chemical, electrical and physiological changes, and emotional changes. How can you refute that the person you are right now, in this moment, is the "same" person 5 minutes ago? You can't! Because of this truth, you are left with only one reality – that what you do is a reflection of who you are – in that moment (remember, *only moments count!*)

Authenticity *is* in each act – the rest is fodder for denial. The presumption of imperfection here frees us up tremendously. We aren't going to act in sync with our most revered values all of the time. There are moments when what we value most is getting rid of some angry energy at someone else's expense. If you believe that only moments count – then you have to accept the reality that in the moment, you may not be who you say you are (or would like to be), but instead, you are what you do! We all have moments of kindness and moments of self-centered selfishness. Those single solitary moments do not define us. However, they are a part of us and are a true reflection of us.

This isn't new. It's just bringing it down to an every day, behavioral level. There is a reason why every major religion holds forgiveness as a major tenet. When we own our actions as an expression of who we authentically were in that moment it keeps our imperfection refreshingly before us. A wise sage once said, "When I looked out at the world I screamed for justice. But when I began to look at myself, I begged for mercy."

Why is this important? Because it opens the door to gratitude and reality, and begins to close the door to arrogance and self-delusion.

When you take the summation of moments – you then are left with a clear articulation of who you are, the most enduring and most disappointing values represented in your behavior. Some say if you want to know what you value take a look at your checkbook and credit card statements. This may be true. However, if we want the broadest picture of what we value, we need only to look at our actions.

It is humbling, freeing and energizing to live in harmony with reality.

PIOOYA mastery is not about taking the easy way out. It is all about dealing in and with reality. It's about holding ourselves accountable. "Fake it till you make it" is a great training program for developing distance from authenticity. After you "make it", what then, be authentic until you lose it?

So, give yourself the freedom of accepting that you are - the summation of your actions. We strive to have our actions more consistent with what we explicitly value, yet our humanity continues to get in the way. When we accept that authenticity is in each act we can only become more deeply comfortable with the reality we operate within. Piooya mastery demands that the final myths about who we are be gently shed in favor of the wonderful truth of our ongoing humanity.

PIOOYA's Time

We have to return to the beginning of this story, the foundation of this journey. At no other time have we as a species been in need of some serious **PIOOYA mastery**. We have been on the brink of financial collapse, toeing the line with global war, facing a real possibility of a number of disease pandemics, over-population and famine. WE NEED SOME SERIOUS PIOOYA if we are going to create a world of greater individual and global freedom and responsibility.

But that's on the macro level.

On the micro level, the need might be even greater. If necessity is the mother of invention and the unemployed in the U.S. alone hovering near 10 million, there should be an abundance of Einsteinian energy buzzing all around. Instead, you find long lines at job fairs and even longer lines at the unemployment and welfare offices. We have OD'd on the opium of looking to others for the answers when we had them all along.

PIOOYA can be messy at times, can feel uncomfortable and outright painful - but in the end, we are healthier, wealthier (in spirit) and much lighter. Ultimately, PIOOYA both frees and fuels the spirit.

The question has never been whether or not you are a Piooya Master – but rather…when will you allow your PIOOYA mastery to emerge?

As fellow travelers, we wish you well.

About the Authors

Bill, a psychologist currently living in Minneapolis, grew up in the east coast metroplex with a dad who took the bus and trolley into Newark each day and a mom who stayed home and took care of the three boys. It was a time marked by elementary school "air raid" drills, when families had two parents and a single car. The senior citizen of the writing duo, Bill brings the maturity to this effort that I completely lack.

After completing graduate school in psychology Bill spent a few years working with troubled kids in the public schools before beginning a therapy and consulting practice that is still active today. The focus of the consulting efforts has been to transform different perspectives into focused action through activities such as strategic planning, facilitation and building high performing teams. For the last half of his career Bill has specialized in the design and delivery of leadership programs in the for-profit and non-profit sectors.

Bill was a senior trainer with the Blandin Foundation leadership programs when we first met. We've been learning from each other since.

Bill is married for 31 years to his wife Mary. They have a combined family of five children and five grand children, all but one residing in the Twin Cities.

Nehrwr is a consultant and trainer living in Fridley, Minnesota. Growing up on the south side of Chicago in one of the toughest neighborhoods seemed to have prepared him for pretty much anything life has thrown at him. He took two city buses for 1.5 hour commute to and from high school. A chapter degree member in the FFA (yes, a black guy from the south side of Chicago in the FFA!) Nehrwr always had a passion for math and science that he brought with him in his quest for a degree in Engineering at the University of Minnesota.

Until he met Organic Chemistry.

He then decided Math was the route for him. While finishing his undergraduate degree in Math, someone took notice of his ability to engage groups and facilitate difficult conversations. And thus, the trainer extraordinaire was born! Facilitating student learning and later working with educators, Nehrwr ventured away from his nest at the University of Minnesota and began his consulting practice full time. Traveling across the country motivating, educating and inspiring others to learn more about themselves and the world around them – he seems to have found his calling.

Well, he's at least convinced himself anyway.

Nehrwr is the youthful spirit of the team whose curiosity led us on the quest for the PIOOYA Principles.